T0084148

GRAPHIC BIOGRAPHIES

WILMA RUDOLPH
Olympic Track Star

by Lee Engfer
illustrated by Cynthia Martin
and Anne Timmons

Consultant:
Billie Luisi-Potts, Executive Director
National Women's Hall of Fame
Seneca Falls, New York

Capstone press

Mankato, Minnesota

Graphic Library is published by Capstone Press,
1710 Roe Crest Drive, North Mankato, Minnesota 56003.
www.capstonepub.com

Library of Congress Cataloging-in-Publication Data
Engfer, Lee, 1963–
Wilma Rudolph: olympic track star / by Lee Engfer; illustrated by Cynthia Martin and Anne Timmons.
p. cm.—(Graphic library. Graphic biographies)
Includes bibliographical references and index.
ISBN: 978-0-7368-5489-4 (hardcover)
ISBN: 978-0-7368-6888-4 (softcover pbk.)
1. Rudolph, Wilma, 1940– —Juvenile literature. 2. Runners (Sports)—United States—Biography—Juvenile literature. 3. Women runners—United States—Biography—Juvenile literature. I. Martin, Cynthia. II. Timmons, Anne. III. Title. IV. Series.
GV1061.15.R83E54 2006
796.42'092—dc22 2005024500

Summary: In graphic novel format, tells the life story of Wilma Rudolph, hero of the 1960 Rome Olympics.

Art Director
Jason Knudson

Designer
Bob Lentz

Storyboard Artist
Bob Lentz

Production Artist
Alison Thiele

Colorist
Cynthia Martin

Editor
Tom Adamson

Editor's note: Direct quotations from primary sources are indicated by a yellow background.

Direct quotations appear on the following pages:
Pages 8, 10, 13, 14 (Mae's 2nd line), 17, 18, 22, 24, 25, from *Wilma* by Wilma Rudolph (New York: New American Library, 1977).
Page 14 (Mae's 1st line), from *Wilma Rudolph* (VHS) by Andrew Schlessinger (Bala Cynwyd, Penn.: Schlessinger Media, 1995).

Printed and bound in China. 5174

TABLE OF CONTENTS

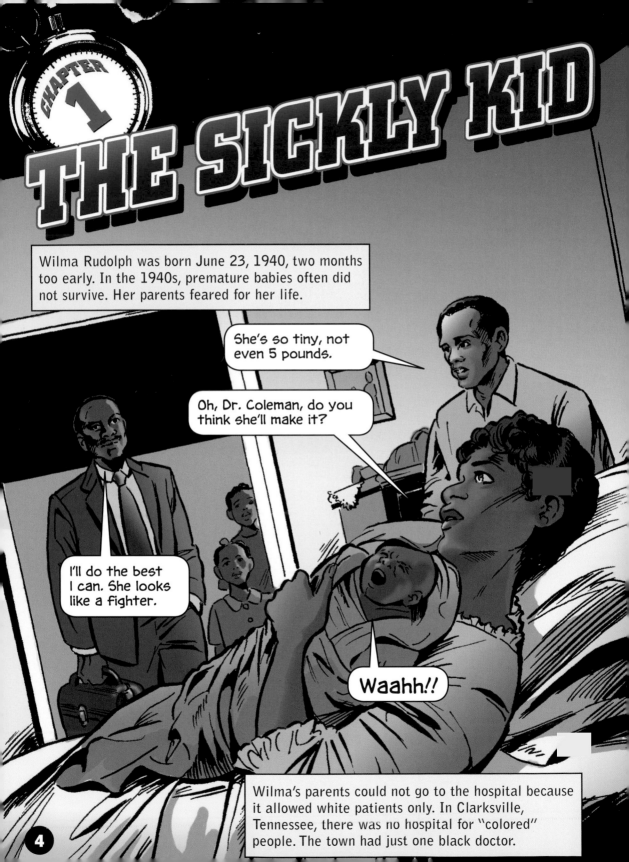

CHAPTER 1 THE SICKLY KID

Wilma Rudolph was born June 23, 1940, two months too early. In the 1940s, premature babies often did not survive. Her parents feared for her life.

She's so tiny, not even 5 pounds.

Oh, Dr. Coleman, do you think she'll make it?

I'll do the best I can. She looks like a fighter.

Waahh!!

Wilma's parents could not go to the hospital because it allowed white patients only. In Clarksville, Tennessee, there was no hospital for "colored" people. The town had just one black doctor.

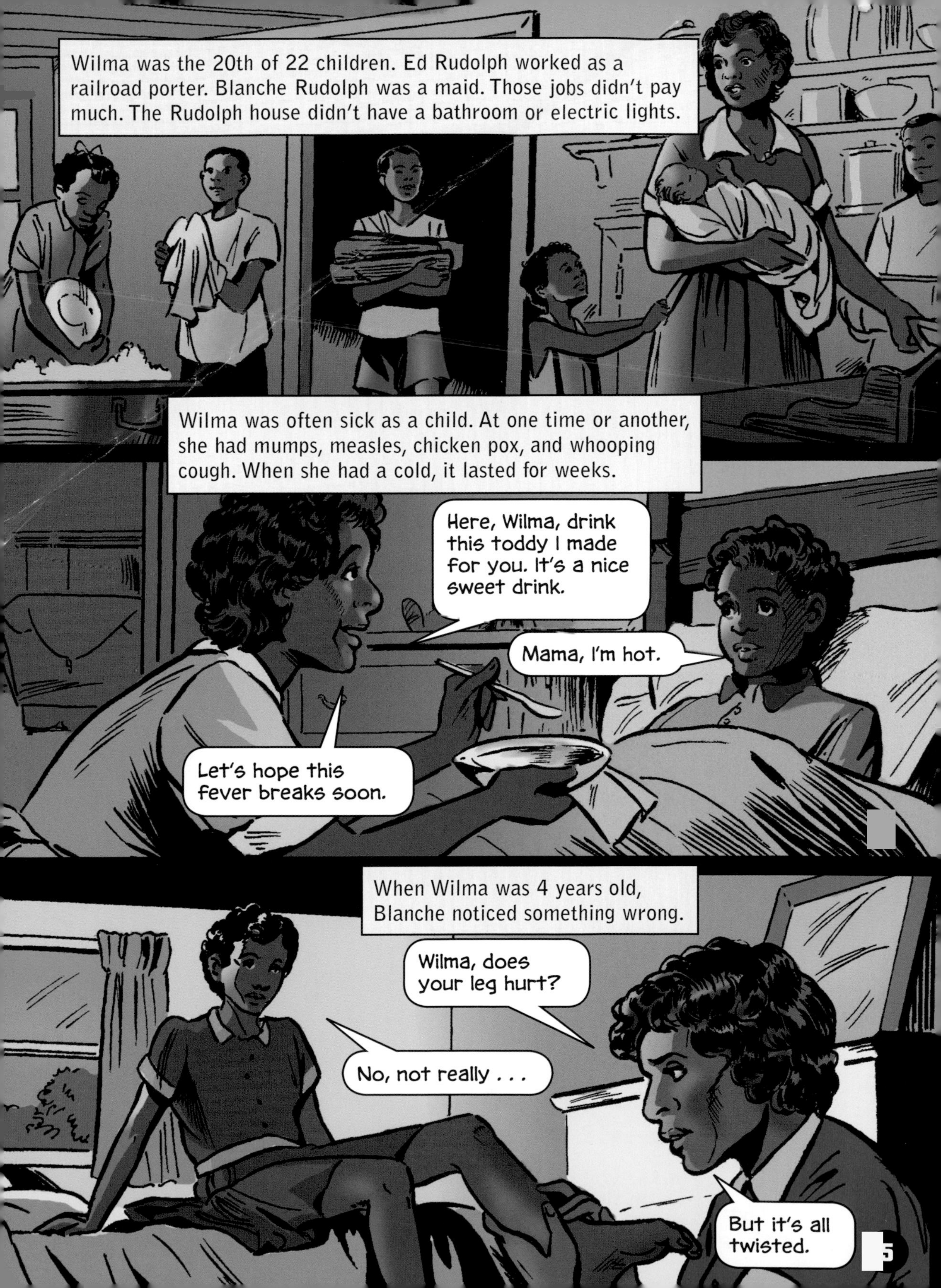
Wilma was the 20th of 22 children. Ed Rudolph worked as a railroad porter. Blanche Rudolph was a maid. Those jobs didn't pay much. The Rudolph house didn't have a bathroom or electric lights.
Wilma was often sick as a child. At one time or another, she had mumps, measles, chicken pox, and whooping cough. When she had a cold, it lasted for weeks.
Here, Wilma, drink this toddy I made for you. It's a nice sweet drink.
Mama, I'm hot.
Let's hope this fever breaks soon.
When Wilma was 4 years old, Blanche noticed something wrong.
Wilma, does your leg hurt?
No, not really . . .
But it's all twisted.
5

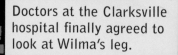

Doctors at the Clarksville hospital finally agreed to look at Wilma's leg.

Wilma must have had polio. It attacks the nerves that control the body's muscles.

She probably will never regain use of her leg.

When Wilma was 6 years old, her mother began taking her to Meharry Medical College. This African American hospital was in Nashville, Tennessee, about 50 miles from Clarksville.

This brace will keep your leg straight, Wilma. Put it on first thing every morning, and don't take it off until you go to bed at night.

Why do you have to do this to my leg?

Wilma, we're going to pull, twist, and massage your leg until it's strong.

The other kids are going to laugh at me.

Would you show me how to do the exercises? I can help with Wilma's treatment at home.

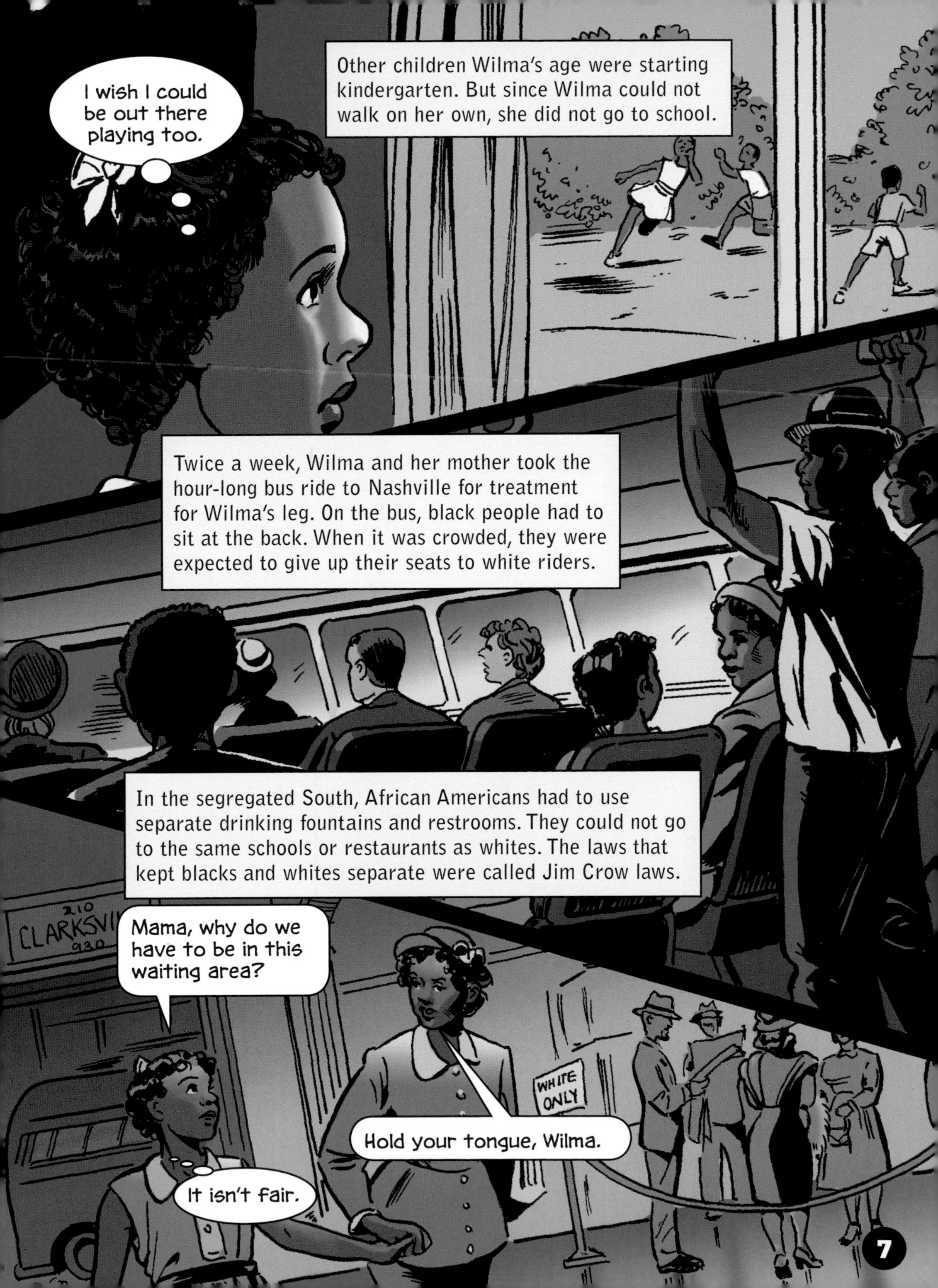
I wish I could be out there playing too.
Other children Wilma's age were starting kindergarten. But since Wilma could not walk on her own, she did not go to school.
Twice a week, Wilma and her mother took the hour-long bus ride to Nashville for treatment for Wilma's leg. On the bus, black people had to sit at the back. When it was crowded, they were expected to give up their seats to white riders.
In the segregated South, African Americans had to use separate drinking fountains and restrooms. They could not go to the same schools or restaurants as whites. The laws that kept blacks and whites separate were called Jim Crow laws.
Mama, why do we have to be in this waiting area?
WHITE ONLY
Hold your tongue, Wilma.
It isn't fair.

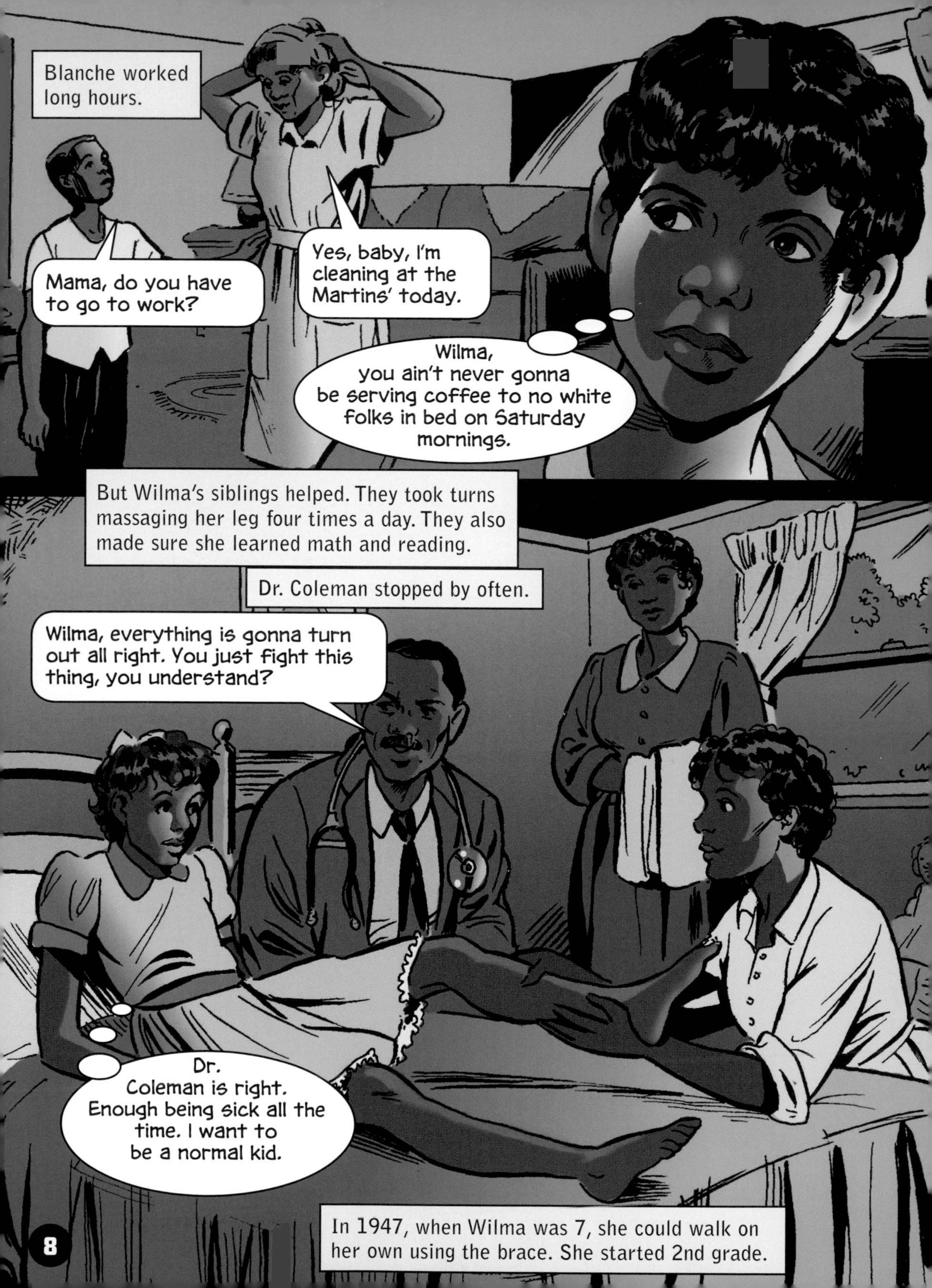
Blanche worked long hours.
Mama, do you have to go to work?
Yes, baby, I'm cleaning at the Martins' today.
Wilma, you ain't never gonna be serving coffee to no white folks in bed on Saturday mornings.
But Wilma's siblings helped. They took turns massaging her leg four times a day. They also made sure she learned math and reading.
Dr. Coleman stopped by often.
Wilma, everything is gonna turn out all right. You just fight this thing, you understand?
Dr. Coleman is right. Enough being sick all the time. I want to be a normal kid.
In 1947, when Wilma was 7, she could walk on her own using the brace. She started 2nd grade.

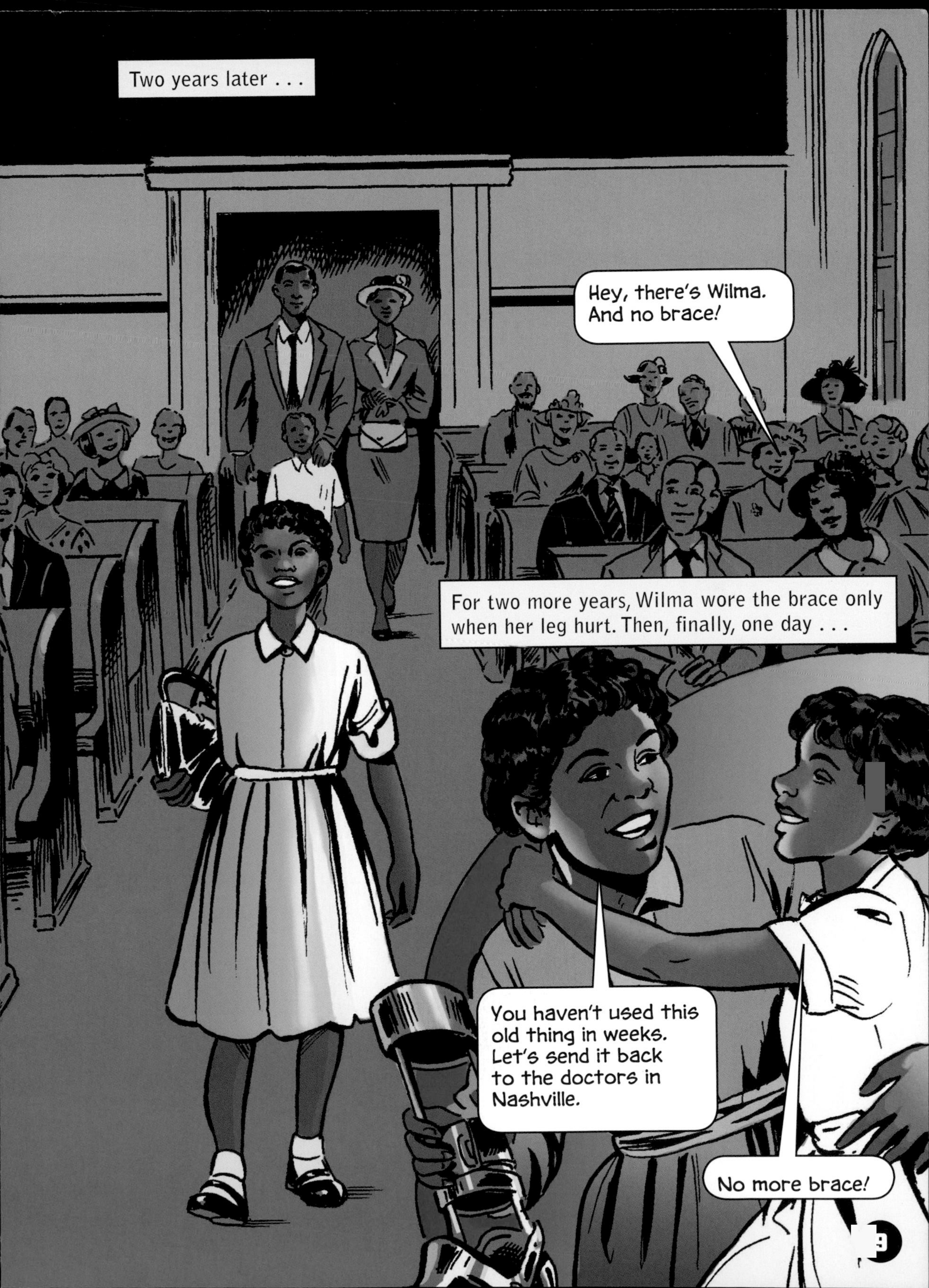
Two years later . . .
Hey, there's Wilma. And no brace!
For two more years, Wilma wore the brace only when her leg hurt. Then, finally, one day . . .
You haven't used this old thing in weeks. Let's send it back to the doctors in Nashville.
No more brace!

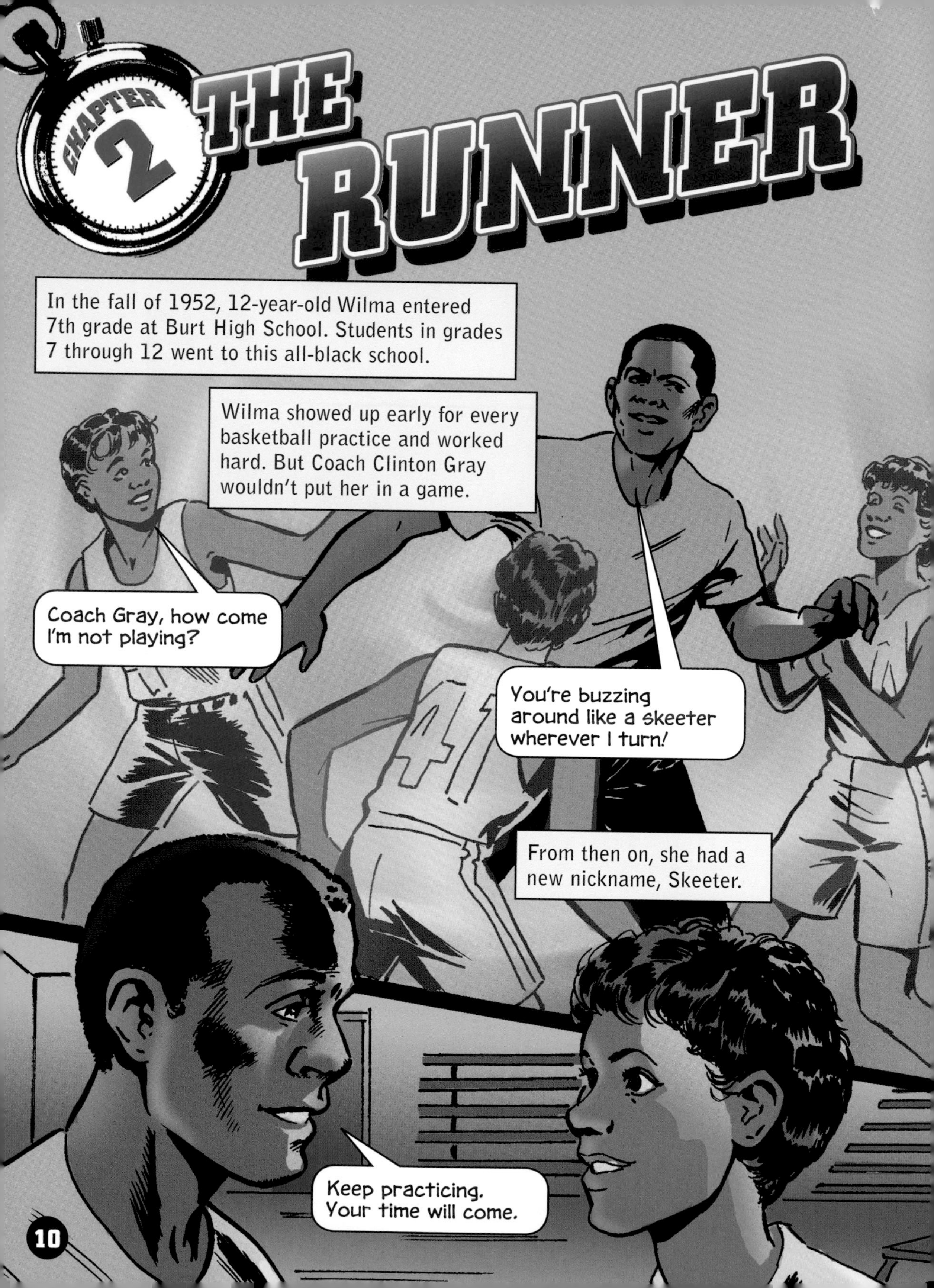

CHAPTER 2
THE RUNNER
In the fall of 1952, 12-year-old Wilma entered 7th grade at Burt High School. Students in grades 7 through 12 went to this all-black school.
Wilma showed up early for every basketball practice and worked hard. But Coach Clinton Gray wouldn't put her in a game.
Coach Gray, how come I'm not playing?
You're buzzing around like a skeeter wherever I turn!
From then on, she had a new nickname, Skeeter.
Keep practicing. Your time will come.

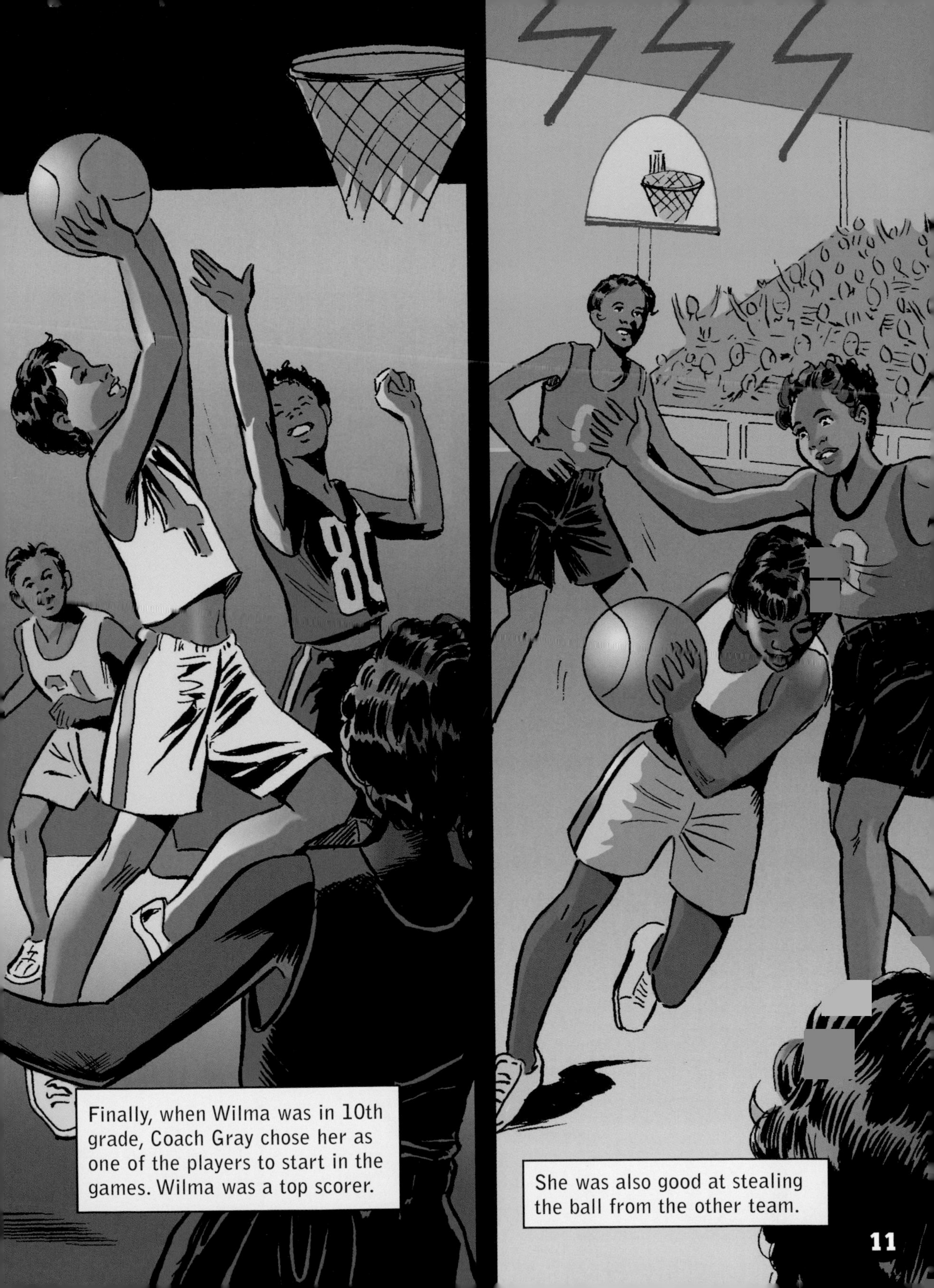
Finally, when Wilma was in 10th grade, Coach Gray chose her as one of the players to start in the games. Wilma was a top scorer.
She was also good at stealing the ball from the other team.

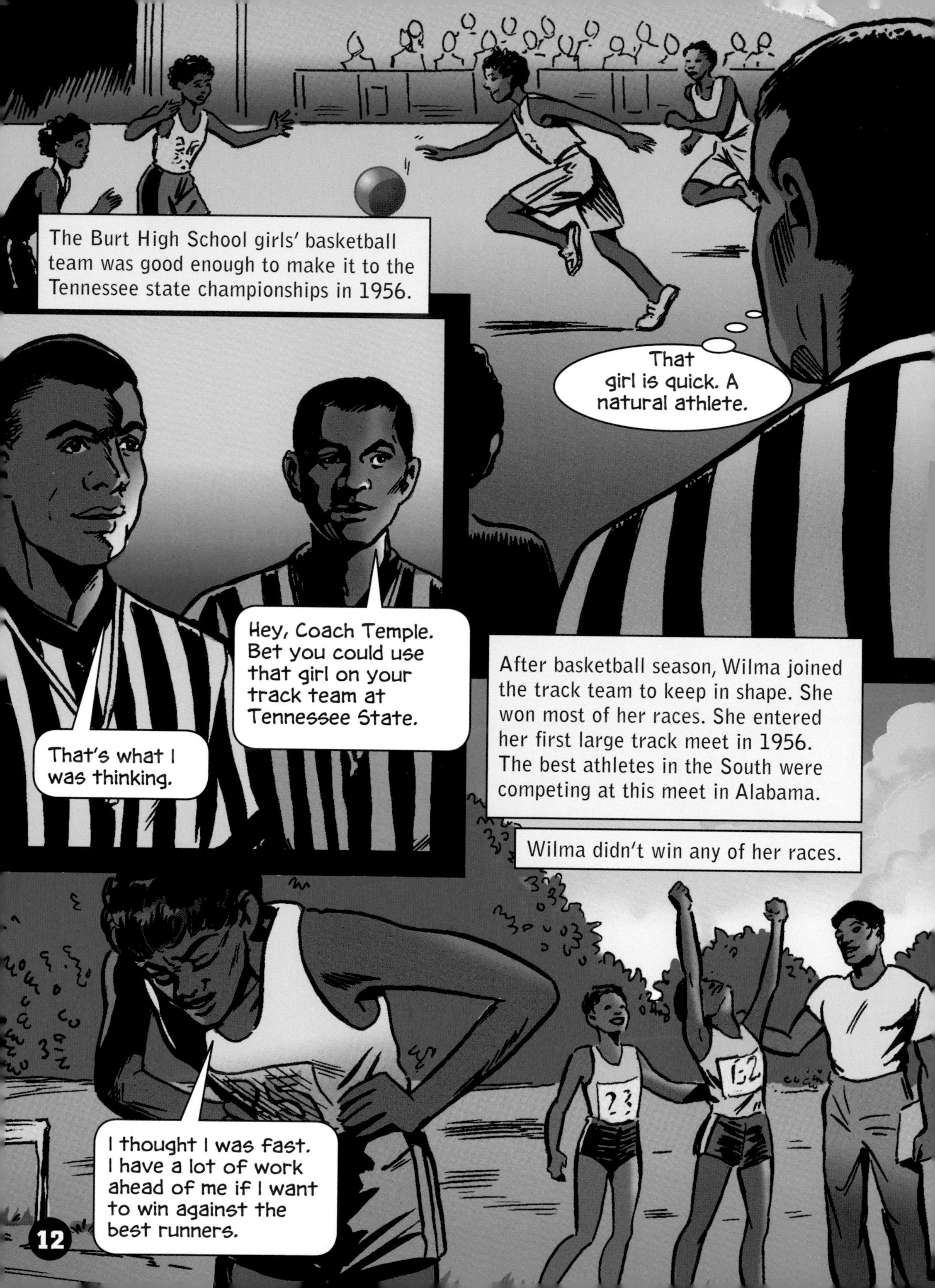

The Burt High School girls' basketball team was good enough to make it to the Tennessee state championships in 1956.
That girl is quick. A natural athlete.
Hey, Coach Temple. Bet you could use that girl on your track team at Tennessee State.
That's what I was thinking.
After basketball season, Wilma joined the track team to keep in shape. She won most of her races. She entered her first large track meet in 1956. The best athletes in the South were competing at this meet in Alabama.
Wilma didn't win any of her races.
I thought I was fast. I have a lot of work ahead of me if I want to win against the best runners.

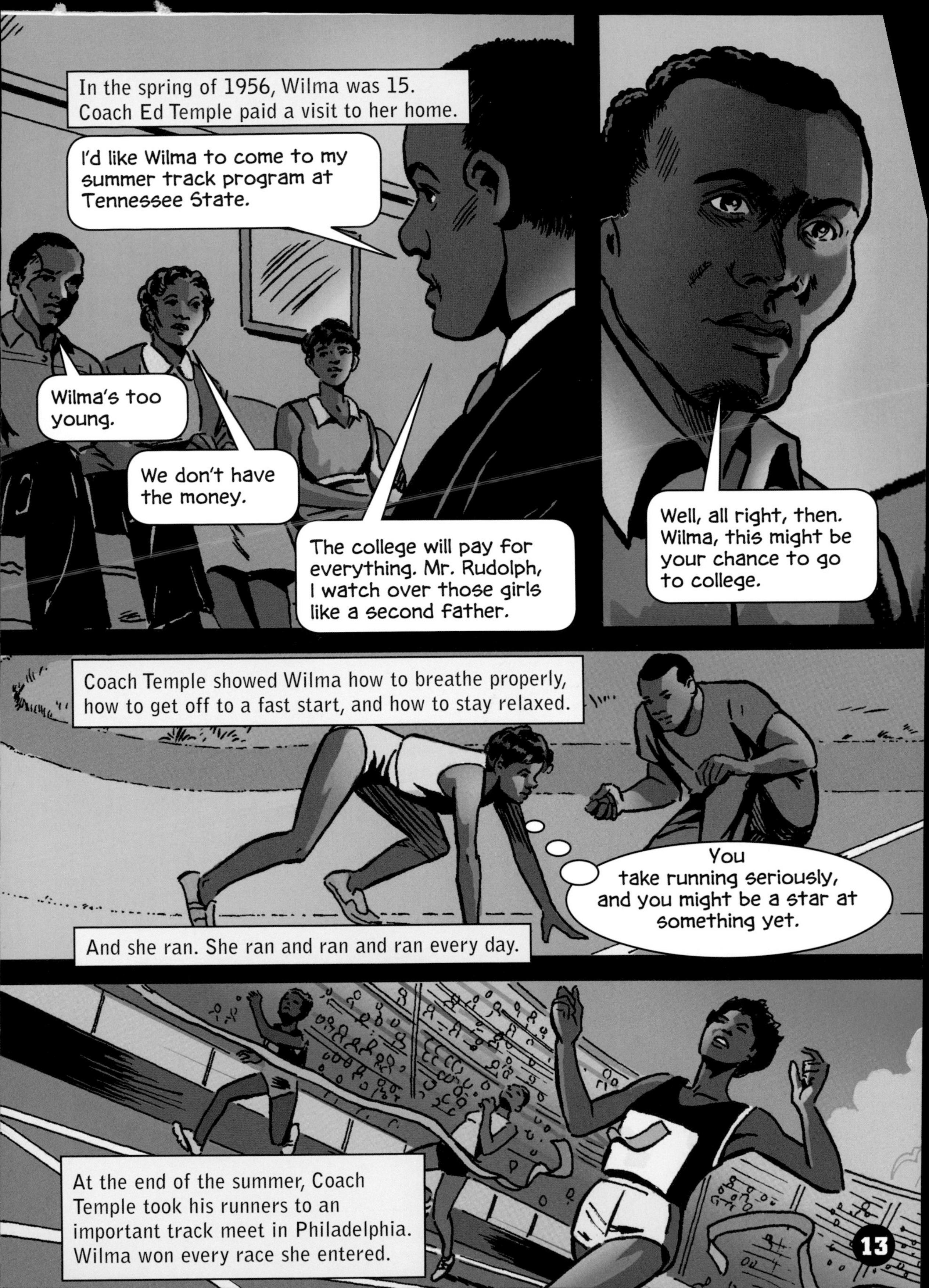

In the spring of 1956, Wilma was 15. Coach Ed Temple paid a visit to her home.
I'd like Wilma to come to my summer track program at Tennessee State.
Wilma's too young.
We don't have the money.
The college will pay for everything. Mr. Rudolph, I watch over those girls like a second father.
Well, all right, then. Wilma, this might be your chance to go to college.
Coach Temple showed Wilma how to breathe properly, how to get off to a fast start, and how to stay relaxed.
You take running seriously, and you might be a star at something yet.
And she ran. She ran and ran and ran every day.
At the end of the summer, Coach Temple took his runners to an important track meet in Philadelphia. Wilma won every race she entered.

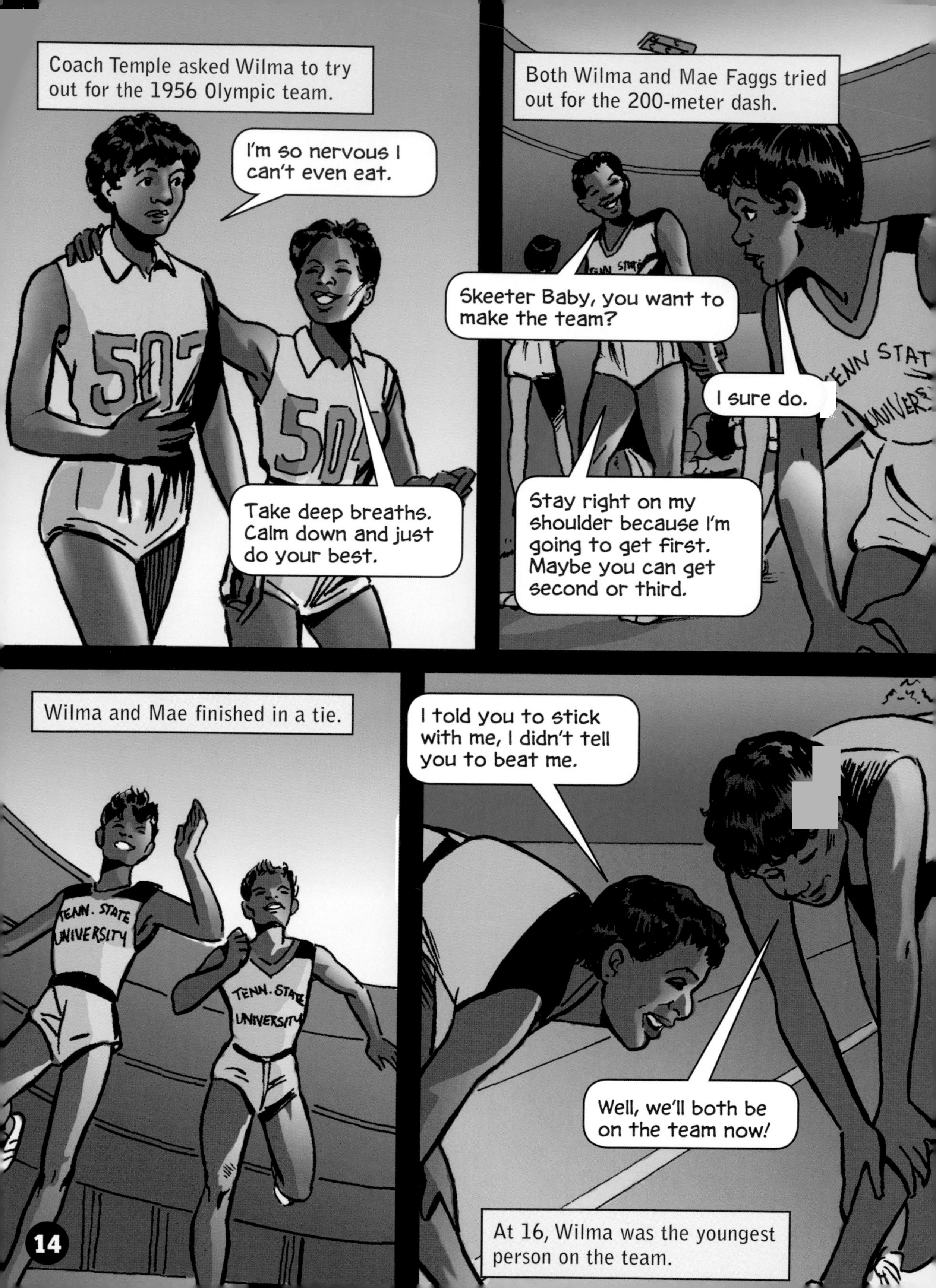

Coach Temple asked Wilma to try out for the 1956 Olympic team.
I'm so nervous I can't even eat.
Take deep breaths. Calm down and just do your best.
Both Wilma and Mae Faggs tried out for the 200-meter dash.
Skeeter Baby, you want to make the team?
I sure do.
Stay right on my shoulder because I'm going to get first. Maybe you can get second or third.
Wilma and Mae finished in a tie.
TENN. STATE UNIVERSITY
TENN. STATE UNIVERSITY
I told you to stick with me, I didn't tell you to beat me.
Well, we'll both be on the team now!
At 16, Wilma was the youngest person on the team.

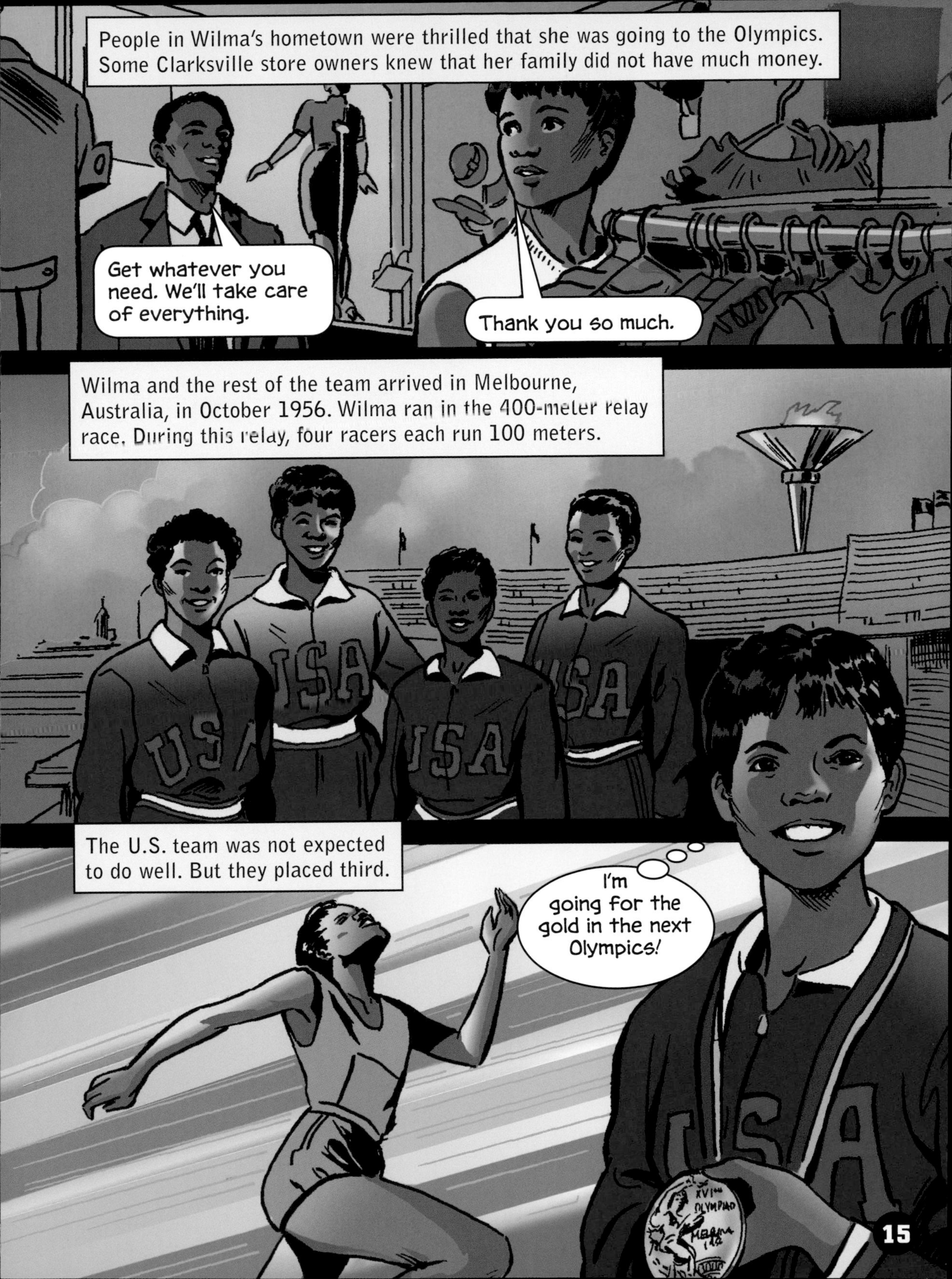
People in Wilma's hometown were thrilled that she was going to the Olympics. Some Clarksville store owners knew that her family did not have much money.
Get whatever you need. We'll take care of everything.
Thank you so much.
Wilma and the rest of the team arrived in Melbourne, Australia, in October 1956. Wilma ran in the 400-meter relay race. During this relay, four racers each run 100 meters.
USA
The U.S. team was not expected to do well. But they placed third.
I'm going for the gold in the next Olympics!

CHAPTER 3
THE 1960 OLYMPICS IN ROME

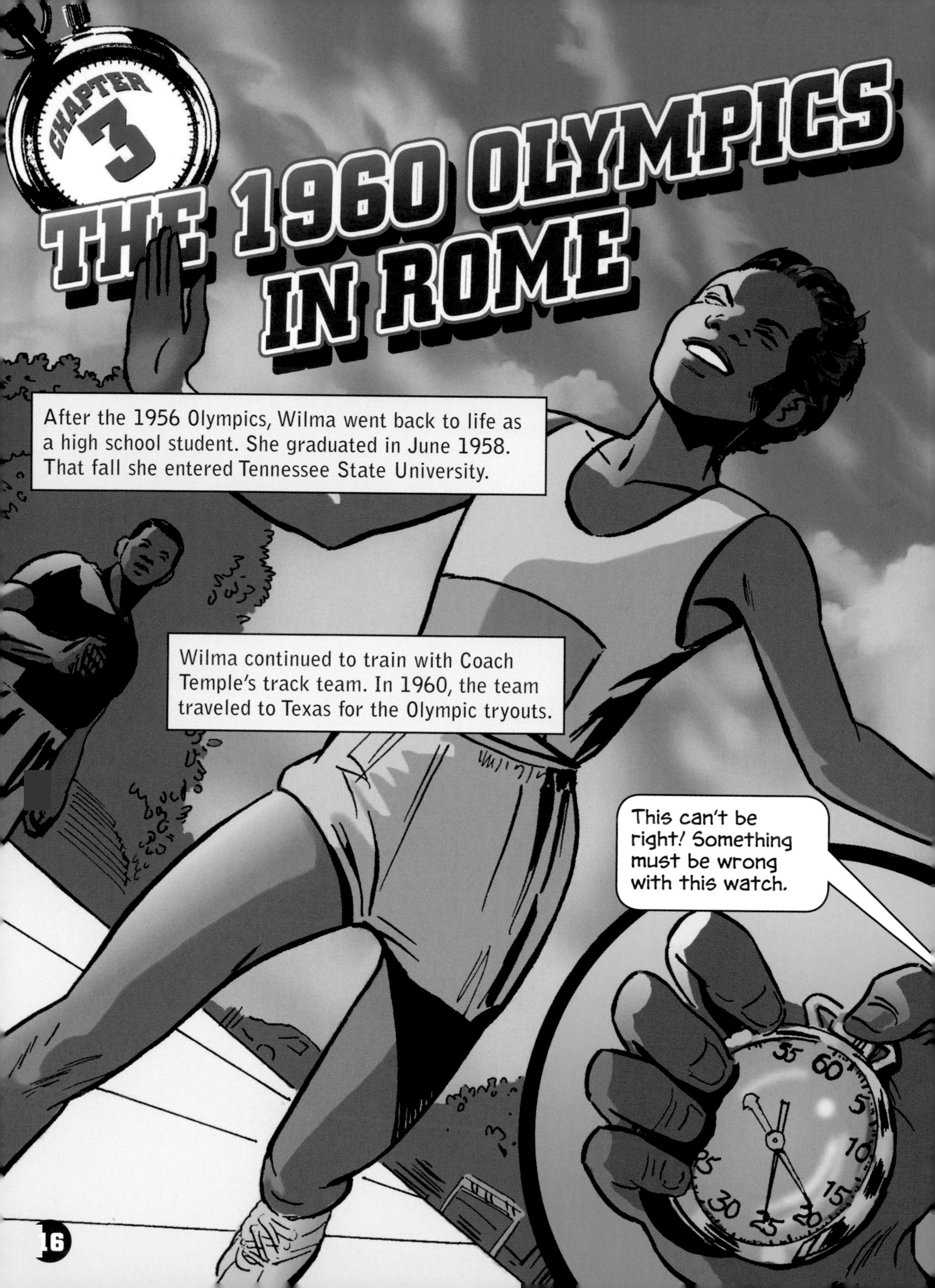
After the 1956 Olympics, Wilma went back to life as a high school student. She graduated in June 1958. That fall she entered Tennessee State University.
Wilma continued to train with Coach Temple's track team. In 1960, the team traveled to Texas for the Olympic tryouts.
This can't be right! Something must be wrong with this watch.

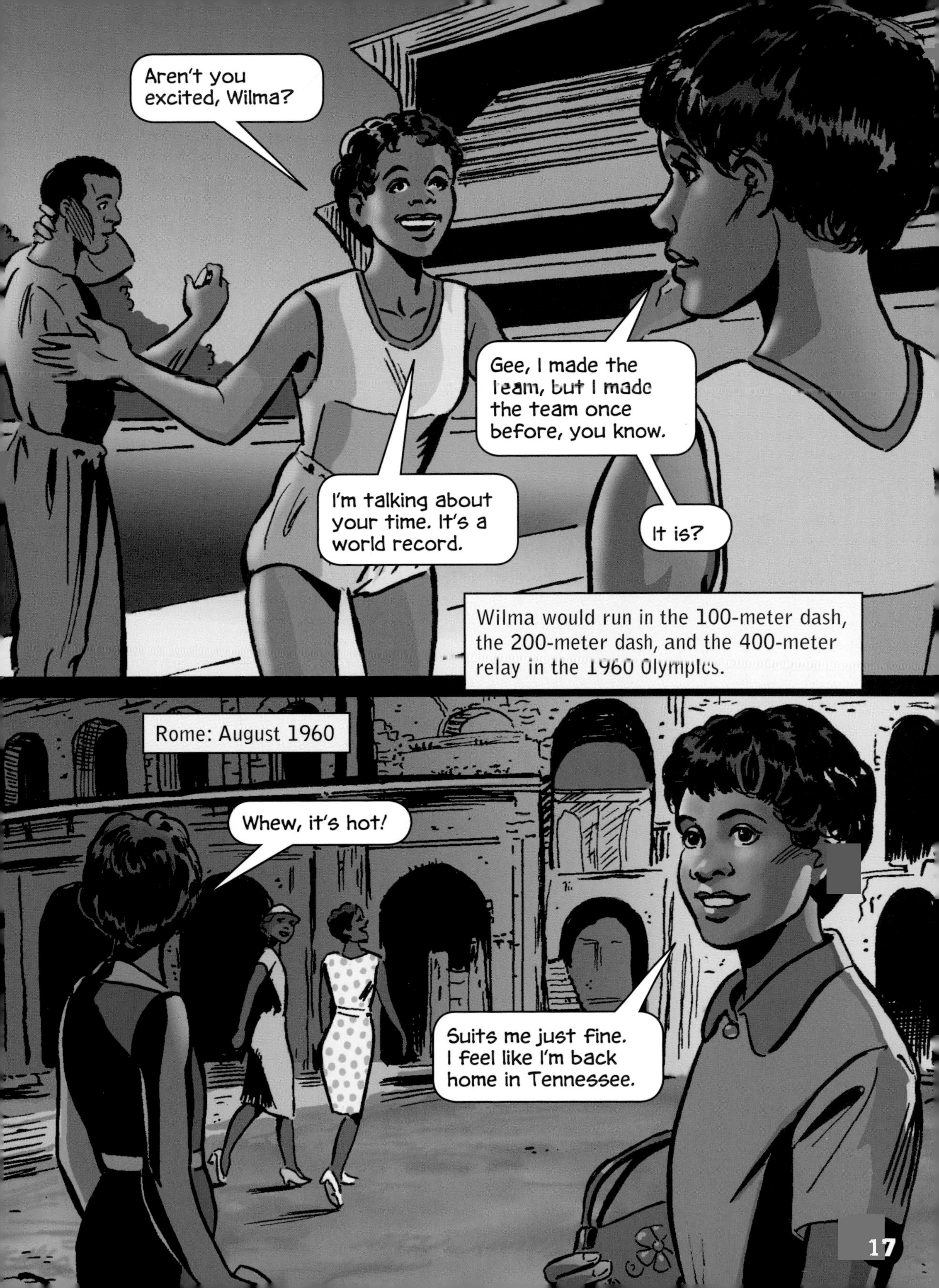
Aren't you excited, Wilma?
Gee, I made the team, but I made the team once before, you know.
I'm talking about your time. It's a world record.
It is?
Wilma would run in the 100-meter dash, the 200-meter dash, and the 400-meter relay in the 1960 Olympics.
Rome: August 1960
Whew, it's hot!
Suits me just fine. I feel like I'm back home in Tennessee.

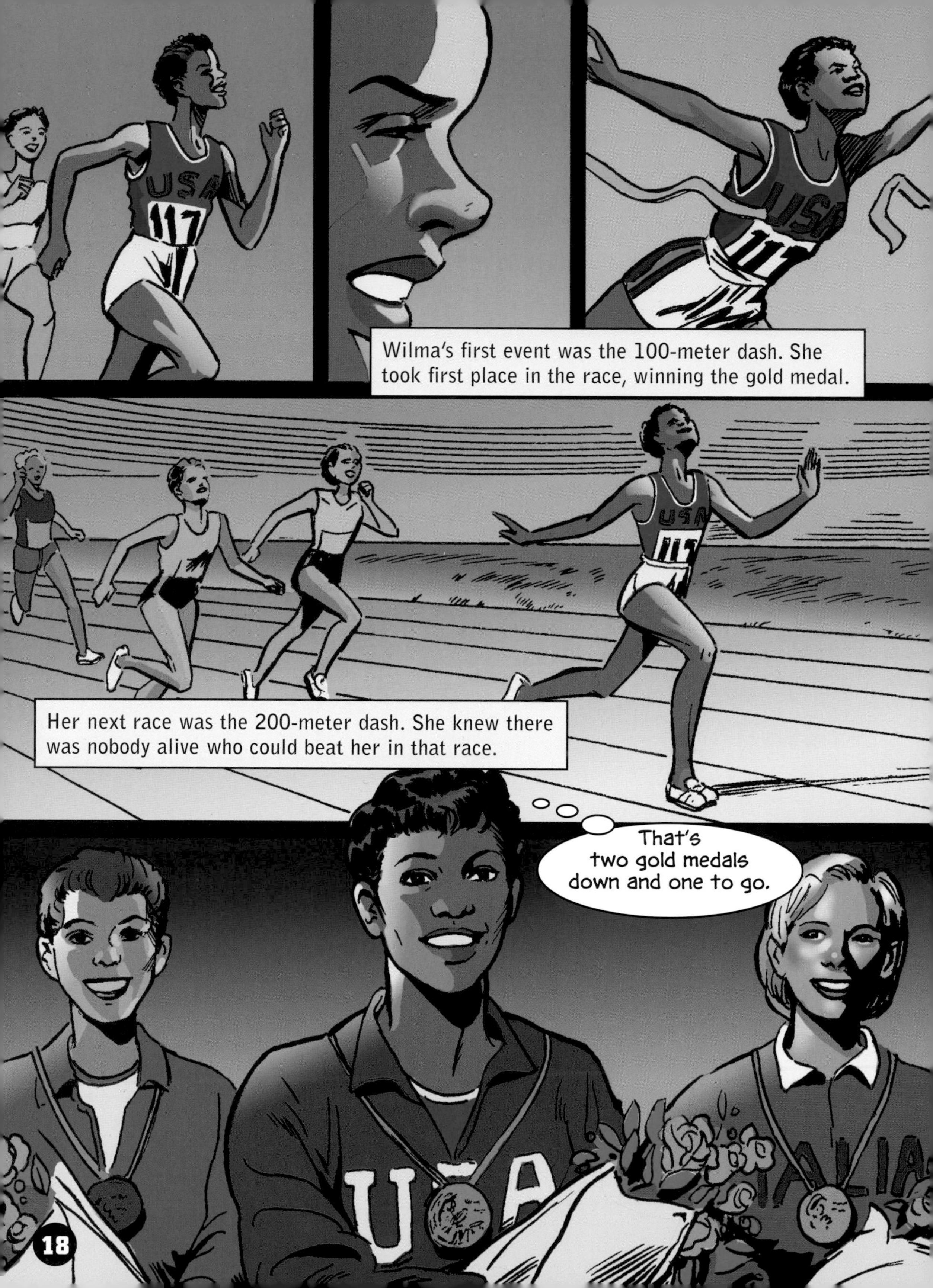

Wilma's first event was the 100-meter dash. She took first place in the race, winning the gold medal.
Her next race was the 200-meter dash. She knew there was nobody alive who could beat her in that race.
That's two gold medals down and one to go.

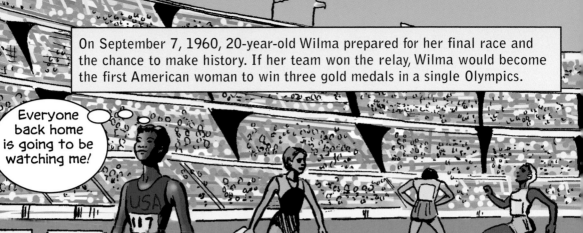

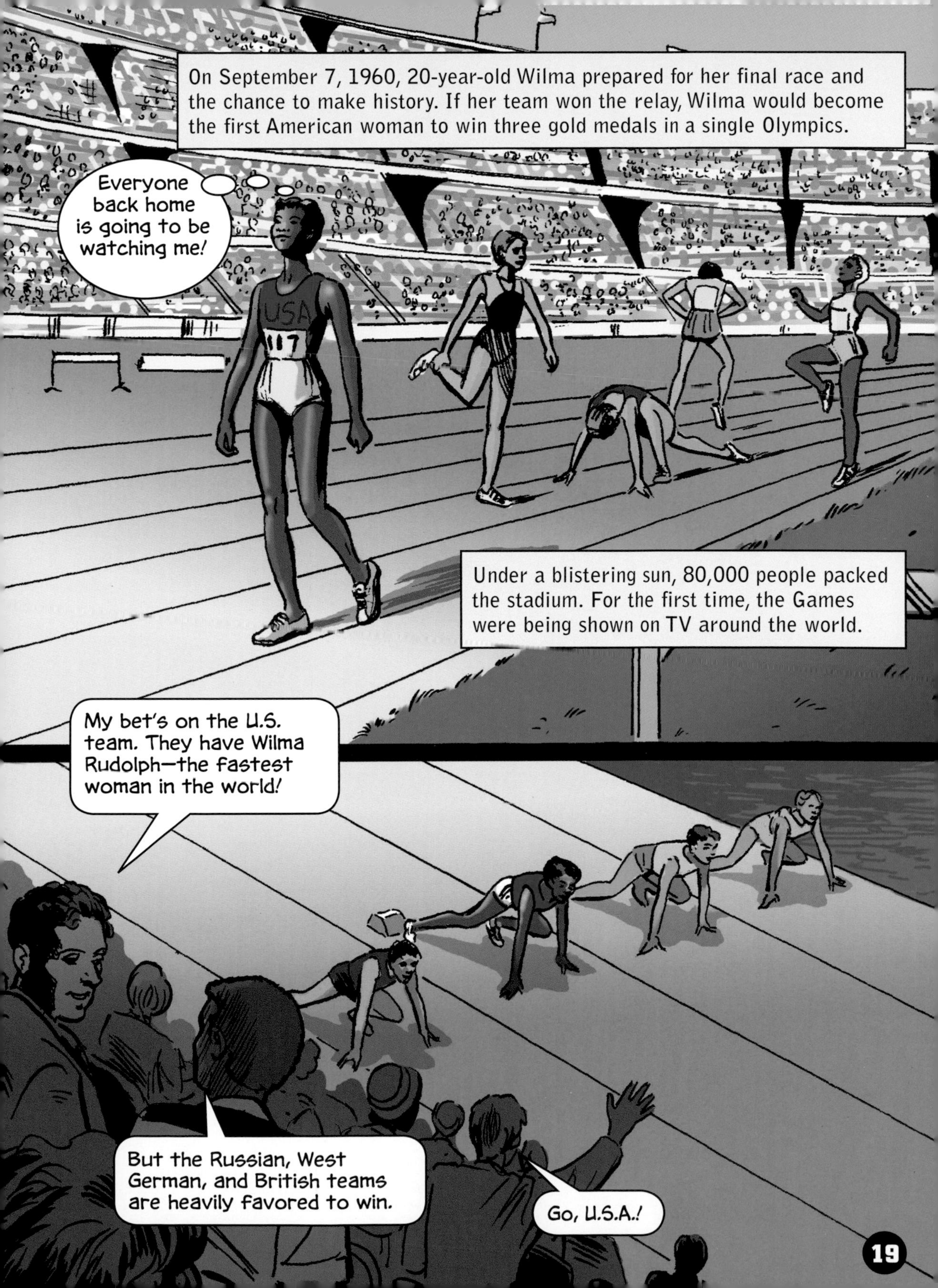

On September 7, 1960, 20-year-old Wilma prepared for her final race and the chance to make history. If her team won the relay, Wilma would become the first American woman to win three gold medals in a single Olympics.

Everyone back home is going to be watching me!

Under a blistering sun, 80,000 people packed the stadium. For the first time, the Games were being shown on TV around the world.

My bet's on the U.S. team. They have Wilma Rudolph—the fastest woman in the world!

But the Russian, West German, and British teams are heavily favored to win.

Go, U.S.A.!

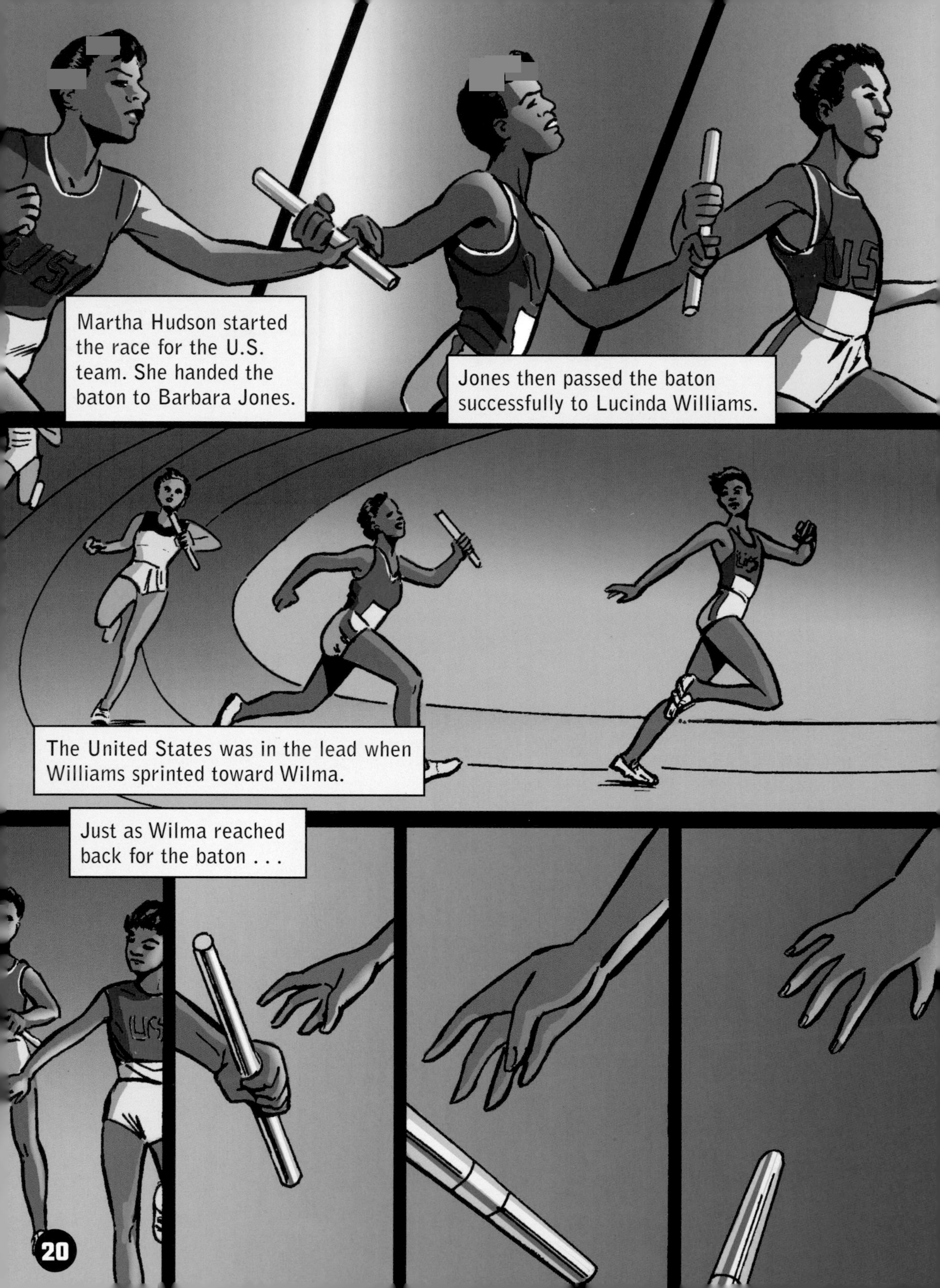

Martha Hudson started the race for the U.S. team. She handed the baton to Barbara Jones.

Jones then passed the baton successfully to Lucinda Williams.

The United States was in the lead when Williams sprinted toward Wilma.

Just as Wilma reached back for the baton . . .

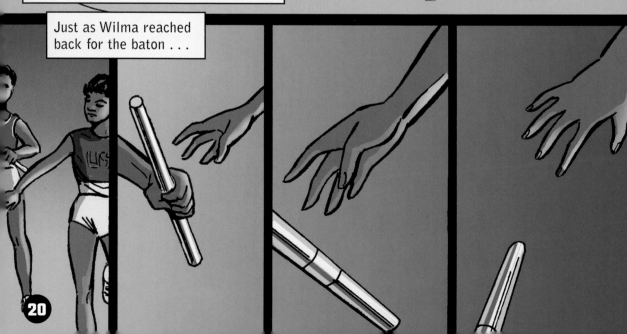

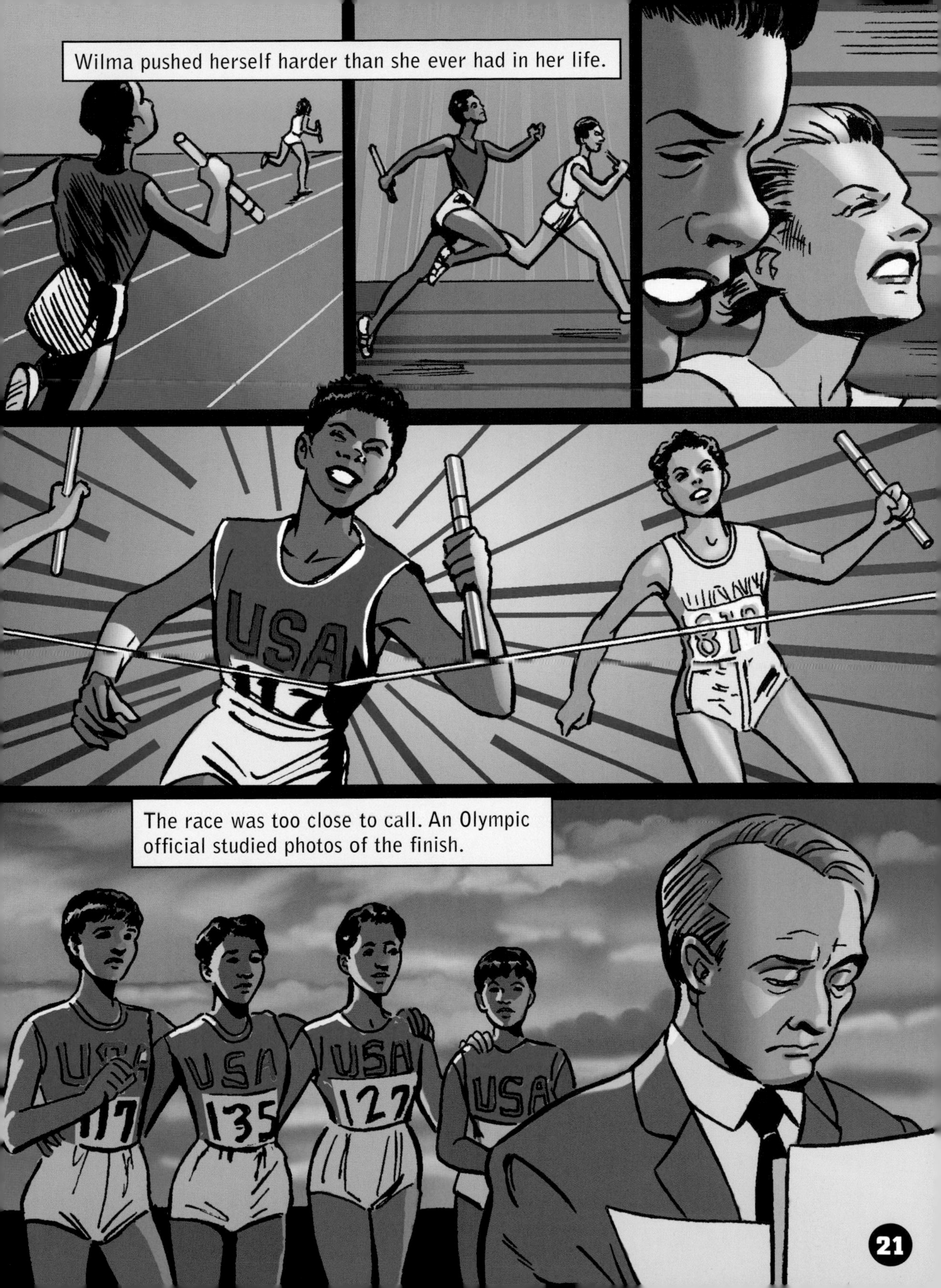
Wilma pushed herself harder than she ever had in her life.
USA
117
The race was too close to call. An Olympic official studied photos of the finish.
USA
117
USA
135
USA
127
USA

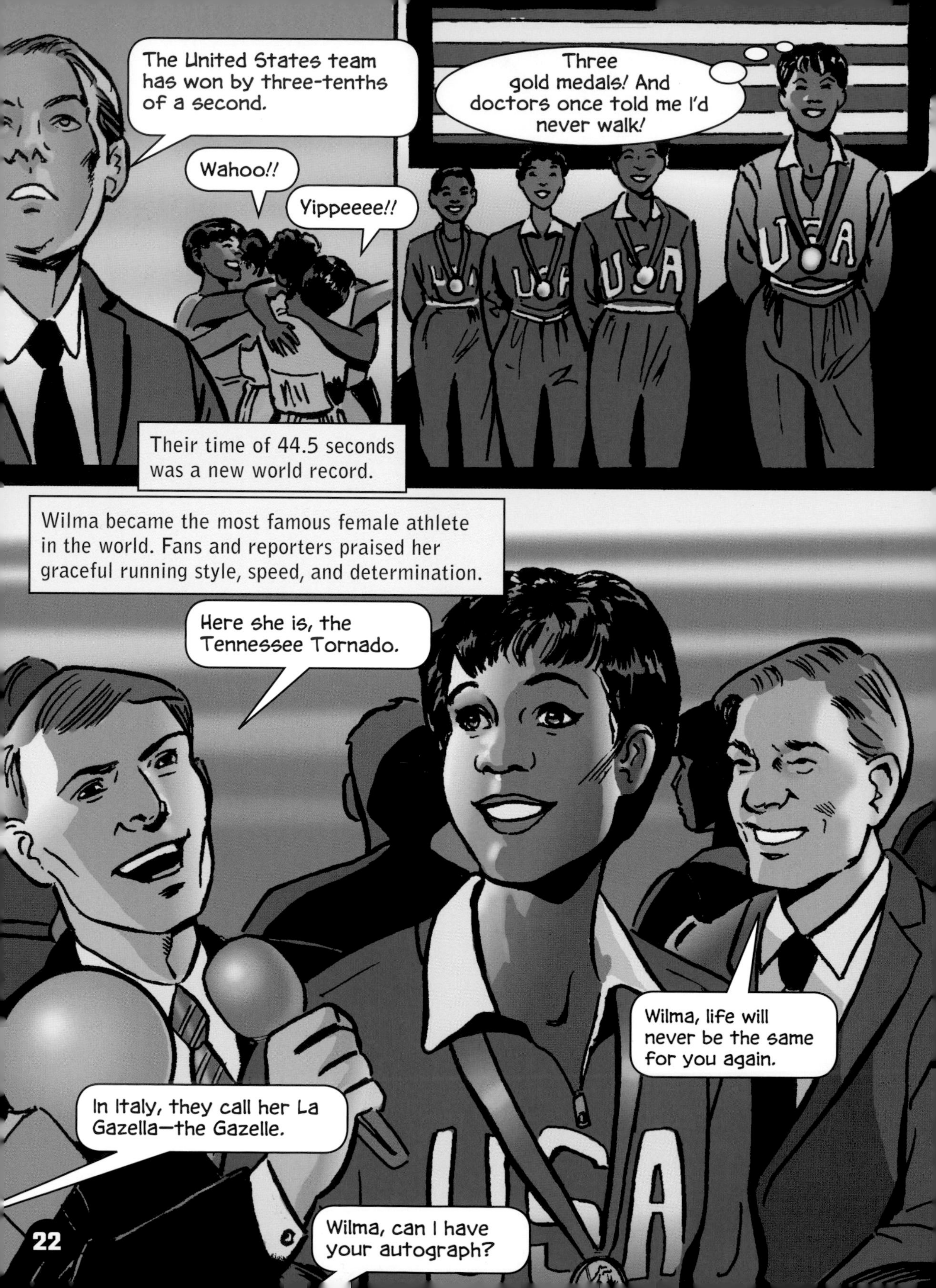
The United States team has won by three-tenths of a second.
Wahoo!!
Yippeeee!!
Three gold medals! And doctors once told me I'd never walk!
Their time of 44.5 seconds was a new world record.
Wilma became the most famous female athlete in the world. Fans and reporters praised her graceful running style, speed, and determination.
Here she is, the Tennessee Tornado.
Wilma, life will never be the same for you again.
In Italy, they call her La Gazella—the Gazelle.
Wilma, can I have your autograph?

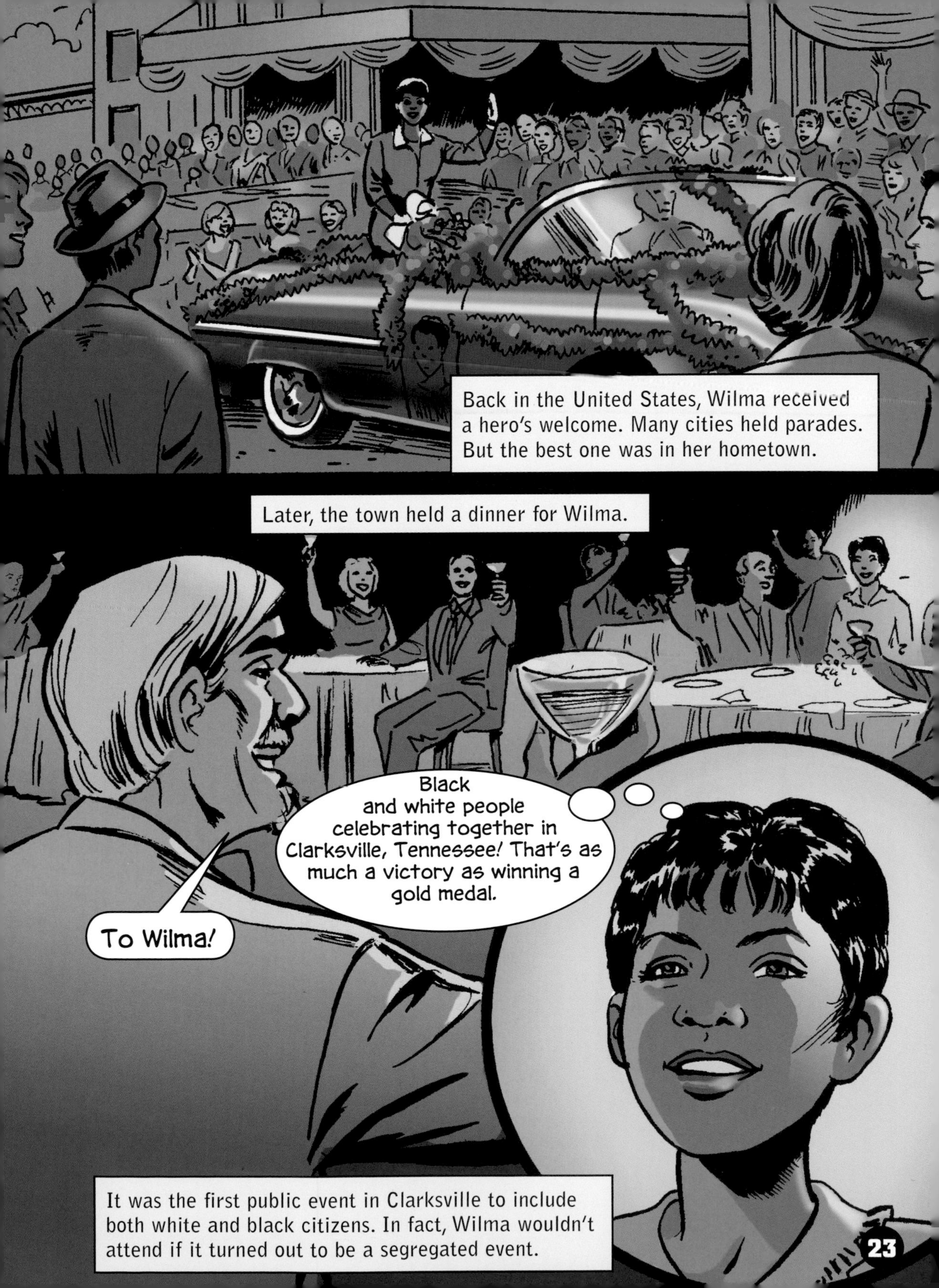
Back in the United States, Wilma received a hero's welcome. Many cities held parades. But the best one was in her hometown.
Later, the town held a dinner for Wilma.
To Wilma!
Black and white people celebrating together in Clarksville, Tennessee! That's as much a victory as winning a gold medal.
It was the first public event in Clarksville to include both white and black citizens. In fact, Wilma wouldn't attend if it turned out to be a segregated event.

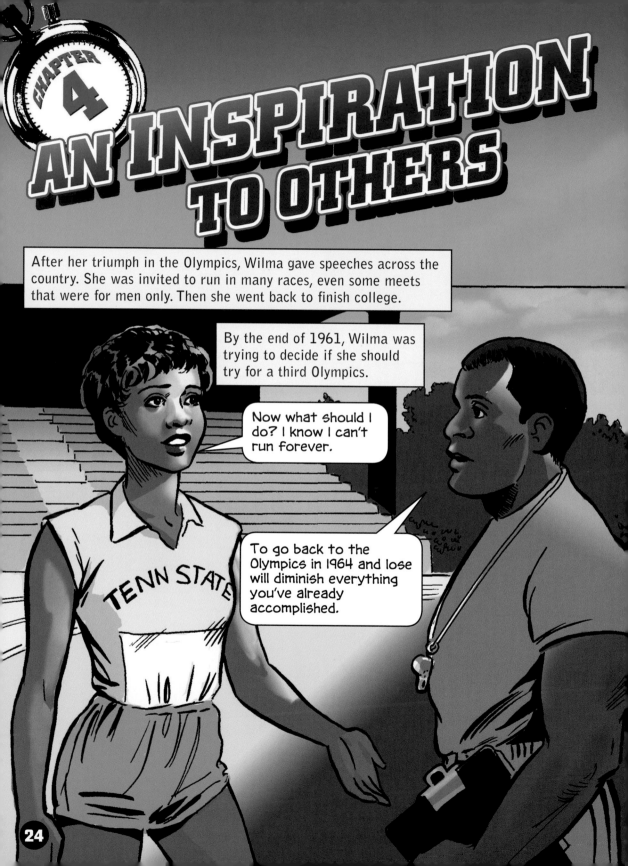

CHAPTER 4

AN INSPIRATION TO OTHERS

After her triumph in the Olympics, Wilma gave speeches across the country. She was invited to run in many races, even some meets that were for men only. Then she went back to finish college.

By the end of 1961, Wilma was trying to decide if she should try for a third Olympics.

Now what should I do? I know I can't run forever.

To go back to the Olympics in 1964 and lose will diminish everything you've already accomplished.

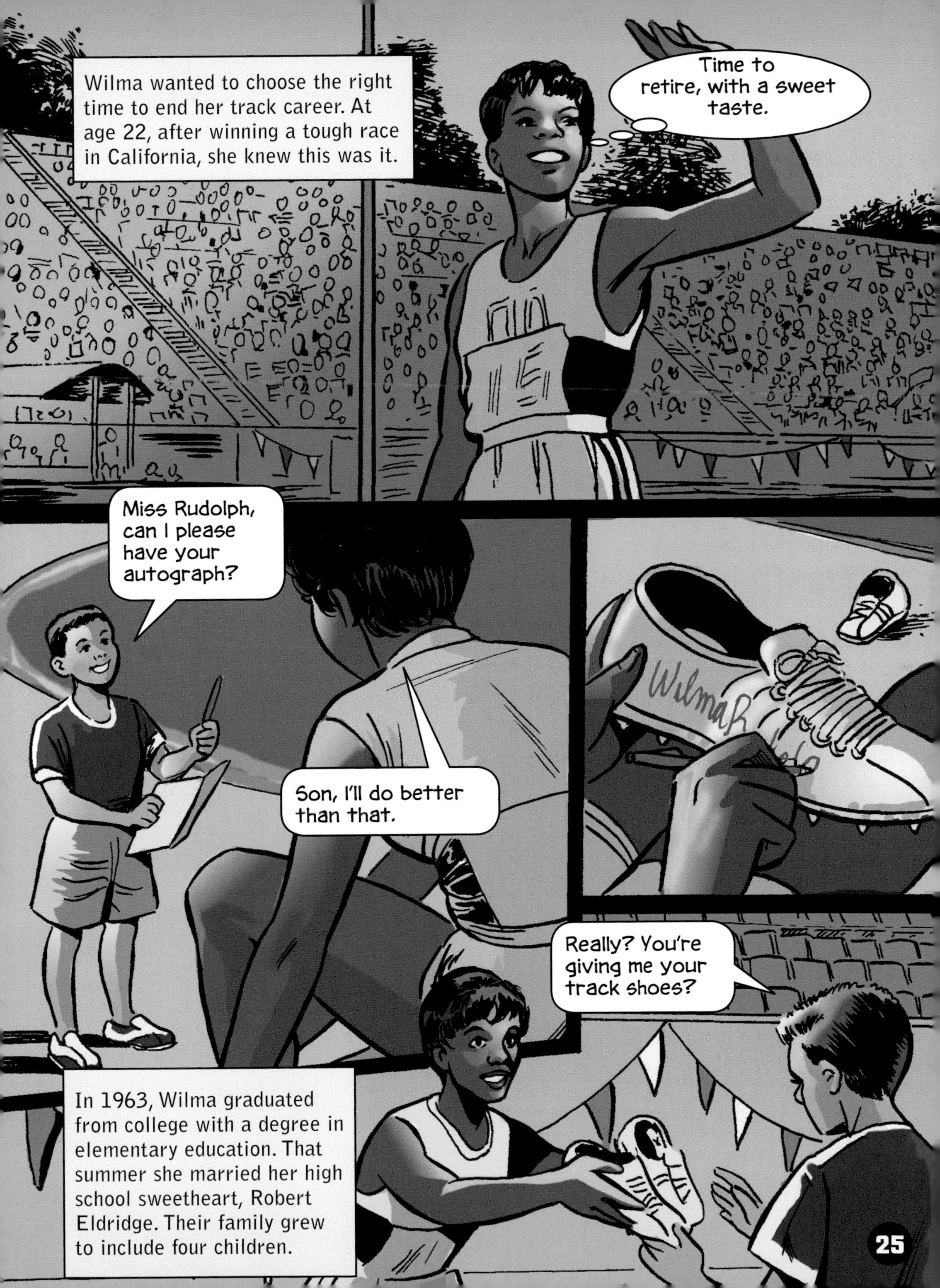
Wilma wanted to choose the right time to end her track career. At age 22, after winning a tough race in California, she knew this was it.
Time to retire, with a sweet taste.
Miss Rudolph, can I please have your autograph?
Son, I'll do better than that.
Really? You're giving me your track shoes?
In 1963, Wilma graduated from college with a degree in elementary education. That summer she married her high school sweetheart, Robert Eldridge. Their family grew to include four children.

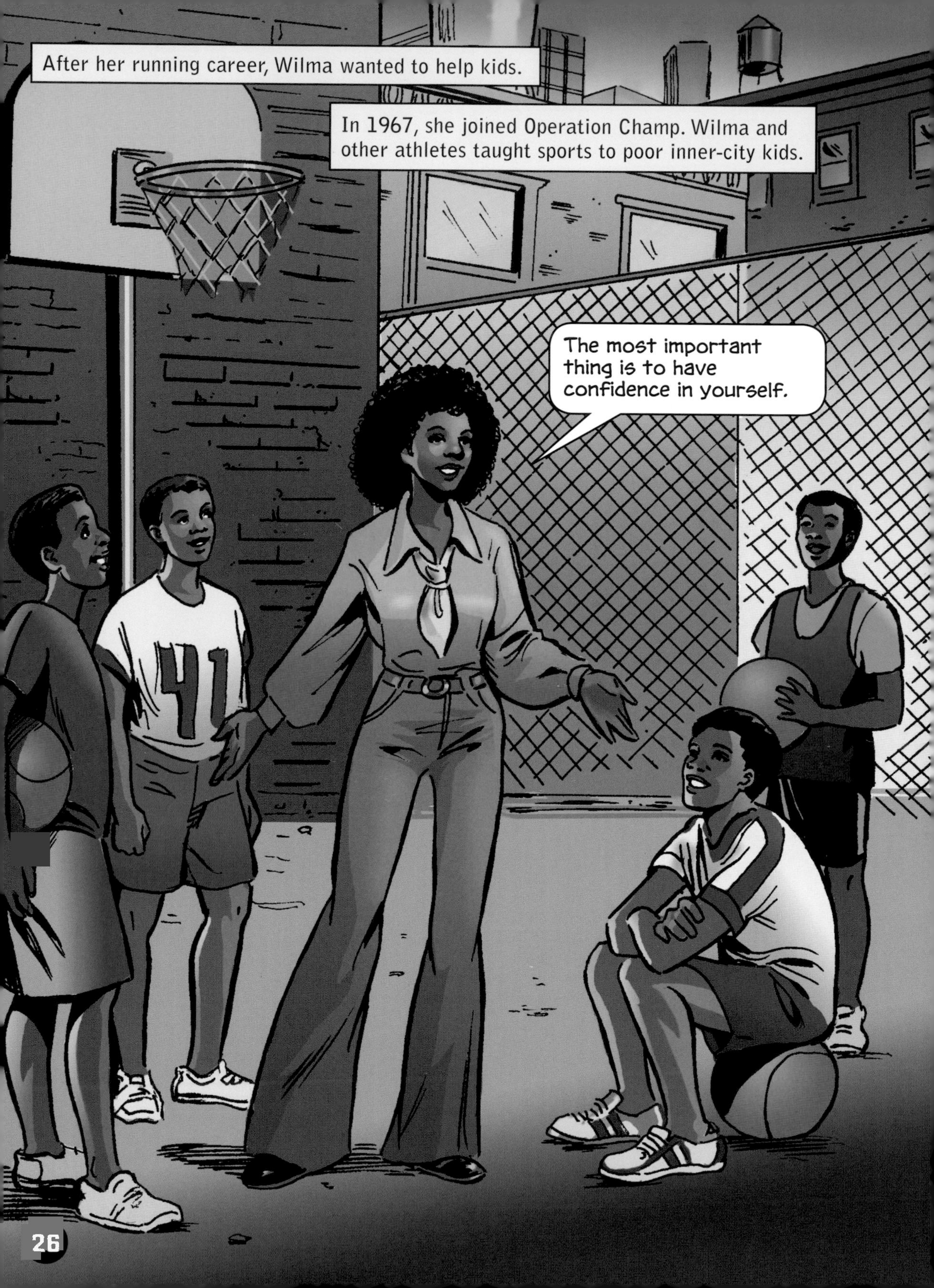
After her running career, Wilma wanted to help kids.
In 1967, she joined Operation Champ. Wilma and other athletes taught sports to poor inner-city kids.
The most important thing is to have confidence in yourself.

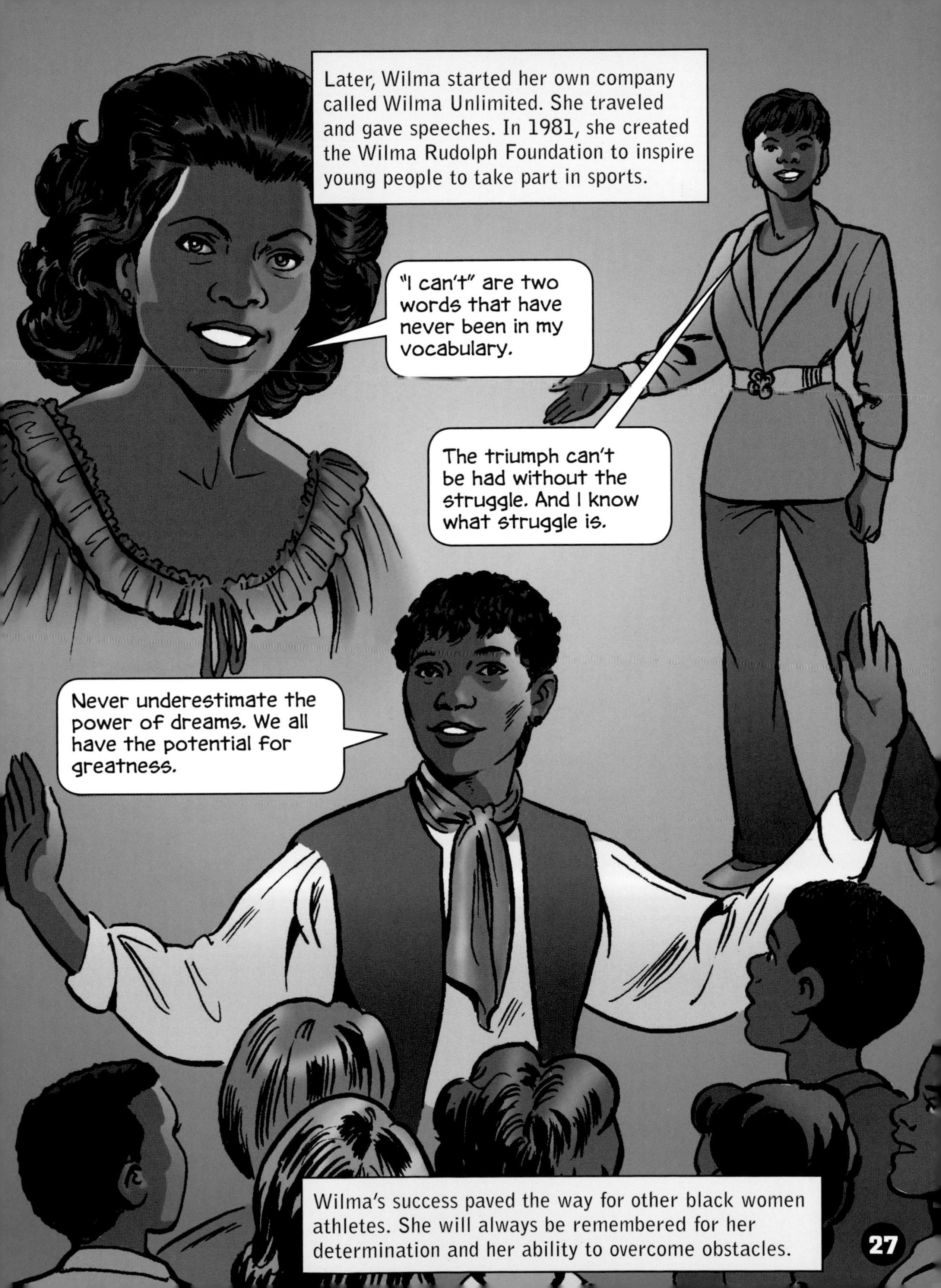
Later, Wilma started her own company called Wilma Unlimited. She traveled and gave speeches. In 1981, she created the Wilma Rudolph Foundation to inspire young people to take part in sports.
"I can't" are two words that have never been in my vocabulary.
The triumph can't be had without the struggle. And I know what struggle is.
Never underestimate the power of dreams. We all have the potential for greatness.
Wilma's success paved the way for other black women athletes. She will always be remembered for her determination and her ability to overcome obstacles.

More about WILMA RUDOLPH

 Wilma Glodean Rudolph was born June 23, 1940.

 Wilma had 21 brothers and sisters. Her father, Ed Rudolph, had 14 children in his first marriage. After he married Blanche, the couple had eight more children.

 In the 1940s, polio struck thousands of children each year. Polio is a virus that spreads just like a cold. The disease causes fever, fatigue, vomiting, and pain in the limbs. One out of every 200 people who got polio became paralyzed. By 1954, polio had killed or crippled more than 350,000 Americans. There is no cure for polio, but a vaccine was invented in 1954, which prevents the disease.

 In 1947, when Wilma started school, black and white students in the South had to go to different schools. States usually gave less money to African American schools. These schools got by with fewer teachers. They had older buildings, books, and equipment. In the 1950s, the U.S. Supreme Court ruled that segregated black schools were not equal to white schools.

- In a tour of Europe after the 1960 Olympics, fans went crazy for Wilma. In Cologne, Germany, police had to hold back the crowd. In Berlin, fans surrounded her bus and beat on it with their fists until she waved.

- Wilma and her husband, Robert Eldridge, had four children: Yolanda, Djuana, Robert, and Xurry.

- In 1977, Wilma wrote a book about her life. The book, *Wilma,* was made into a TV movie starring Cicely Tyson and Denzel Washington.

- In 1980, Tennessee State University named its indoor track for Wilma Rudolph. That year she was also named to the Women's Sports Hall of Fame.

- In 1994, Wilma was diagnosed with brain and throat cancer. She died November 12, 1994. She was just 54 years old.

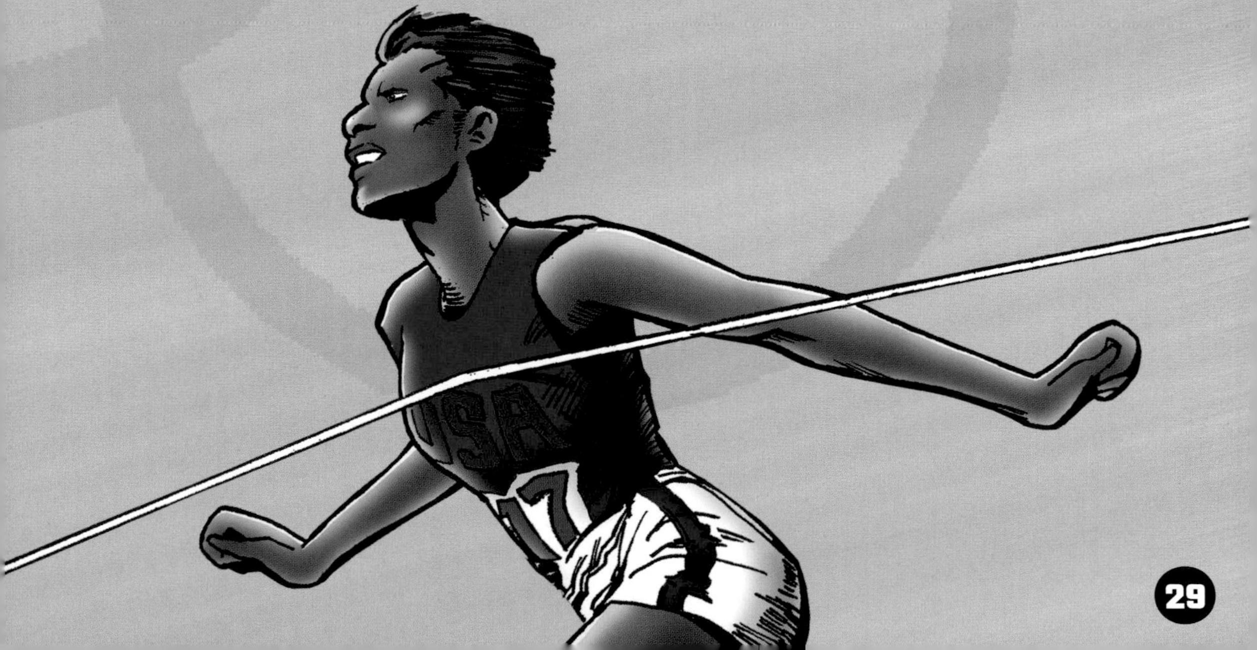
USA
117

GLOSSARY

autograph (AW-tuh-graf)—a person's handwritten signature

dash (DASH)—a short race

determination (de-tur-min-AY-shuhn)—making a decision to accomplish something and not changing your mind

massage (muh-SAHZH)—to rub with the fingers and hands to loosen muscles or to help a person relax

paralyzed (PAIR-uh-lyzed)—unable to move or feel a part of the body

premature (pree-muh-TOOR)—too early

relay (REE-lay)—a race involving a team; each team member covers part of the race. In a 400-meter relay, each runner covers 100 meters.

retire (ri-TIRE)—to give up a line of work

segregated (SEG-ruh-gate-ed)—separated, or forced apart; racial segregation is separation by race.

sprint (SPRINT)—to run fast for a short distance

tryout (TRYE-out)—a test to see if a person is qualified to do something

INTERNET SITES

FactHound offers a safe, fun way to find Internet sites related to this book. All of the sites on FactHound have been researched by our staff.

Here's how:

1. Visit *www.facthound.com*
2. Type in this special code **0736854894** for age-appropriate sites. Or enter a search word related to this book for a more general search.
3. Click on the **Fetch It** button.

FactHound will fetch the best sites for you!